MW01001027

Back to Normal

Back to Normal

RICK FLANDERS
Revival Ministries
6061 Maple Road
Vassar, MI 48768
drrickflanders@gmail.com

All rights reserved. No part of this book may be reproduced in any manner whatsoever without prior written permission except in the case of brief quotations embodied in critical articles or brief reviews.

Back to Normal
Rick Flanders

© 2003 Preach the Word Ministries, Inc.
P. O. Box 242, Menomonee Falls, WI 53052

To order this book call 1-989-863-0784

ISBN 10: 1-933-858-33-8
ISBN 13: 978-1-933858-33-3

Printed in the United States of America

15 14 13 12 11 10 9 8 7 6 5 4 3

DEDICATION

This book is dedicated to Toni, my wonderful wife and partner in the service of the Lord, whose prayers, convictions, and spirituality have immeasurably aided my Christian life.

CONTENTS

FOREWORD

The book you are about to read is good. I know the previous statement will be seen by some as rather simplistic, but it is a good book!

Yes, we could talk about the author. Rick Flanders is, after all, a man who has studied and taught Bible truths about revival most of his life. A pastor in a rural area of Michigan for more than a quarter of a century, Pastor Flanders has a heart that burns for God's people to "return to normal." He is a preacher that teaches the Bible carefully, interestingly, and clearly. He lives what he preaches. He wins people to Christ. He and Toni, his wife, have a beautiful marriage. His own children all love the Lord and are a real plus to the ministry of their parents.

We could talk about the interest in the hearts of thousands of Christians about the matter of revival. It is obvious that a hunger for drawing close to the Savior exists in our circles today. That worldliness and shallow Christian living abound cannot be argued; but with our powerless lives, I sincerely believe you will find among us the desire to be close to the Lord and know His provision and power.

We could talk about the contents of this book. Defining revival might seem a daunting task; there is much misunderstanding out there. However, Dr. Flanders sets the definition in front of us simply and clearly in the first few pages. He answers the questions of a seeking heart and gives substantial evidence to the questioning mind. Is revival an act of God apart from the desires and obedience of His children? Will prayer for revival work? The answers are in the pages you are about to turn. Is revival an ". . . unusual work of God, 'extraordinary' and beyond what can be considered 'normal.'" You are not far from the answer. "Our unbiblical conception of revival points to our great need for it," Dr. Flanders says. This book gives a Bible definition of revival and shows us the way to it.

We could discuss the way this book is written. It is refreshing. Reading what is written here is like opening the door of a dungeon and entering into a beautiful spring day. You are going to enjoy it.

The book you are about to read is good. It is true. It is helpful. It is needed. As you read it, you will sense a growing desire to get back to normal. Our prayer is simply, "Dear Lord, may it be so."

—By Bill Rice III

INTRODUCTION

The great Civil War historian Bruce Catton drew his inspiration to write about the past from memories of his childhood home in Benzonia, Michigan. The intensely religious town had been founded several decades before Catton's birth by revivalists from Ohio.

> Growing up in Benzonia was just a bit like growing up with the Twelve Apostles for next-door neighbors. You never could forget what you were here for . . . no one inherited his faith in our town; abundant testimony showed that God entered your heart only at your own express invitation. The experience was said to be unmistakable, and the true life of the spirit began then and then only. . . . A man knew where he stood. He had a perspective on life that unbelievers did not have.[1]

So the great author remembered a place and time baptized in true revival. Although matriculation in a religiously apostate college altered his morals and choked out much of Catton's simple faith, he always looked back fondly to the excitement and joy he had known breathing the atmosphere of revival.

Revivals of biblical Christianity have had a great effect on American history. It can be argued that our cultural and moral decline in the twentieth century has been due in great part to the decline in the power, extent, and frequency of such revivals. This is one reason for the continuing interest among Christians in the nature and origin of revivals and in what can be done to promote them.

However, there are problems in the quest for revival. Many are confused about what revival truly is. Many others have given up on revival. A great obstacle to revival in our time is the argument over its definition. In order to regain the ground that evangelical Christians have lost over the past hundred years, they must find again and preach again the biblical definition of revival: coming back to normal. When God answers the prayer of believers to "revive us again," He restores them to the level of spirituality that the New Testament presents as normal for Christians. Sadly, we have too long regarded the "usual" as the "normal" and have treated revival as something supernormal for the church.

When present-day disciples of Jesus Christ realize that the powerful experience of the first-century believers, of the eighteenth-century Moravians, of the American Great Awakenings, and of the Welsh Revival represents what happens when New Testament Christianity is lived at its normal level, we will pray and preach for revival with renewed confidence and vigor. It is the object of this book to encourage us in that direction.

NOTE

[1]Bruce Catton, *Waiting for the Morning Train: An American Boyhood* (Garden City, New York: Doubleday and Co., 1972), pp. 23-24, 26, 29.

CHAPTER 1

What Is a Revival?

Wilt thou not revive us again: that thy people may rejoice in thee? (Psalm 85:6)

There is an important discussion occurring today about the subject of spiritual revival. The nature and causes of a revival are being analyzed and explained from several points of view among evangelicals and fundamentalists. To some, a revival of biblical Christianity comes as a surprise from Heaven, an unusual and unpredictable event sent as a sovereign act of God. Others hold the more hopeful view that God revives His people in response to their repentance and prayer. The Hebrew word for "revive" appears in many Old Testament prayers and points to something experienced by believers of all eras. This word helps us to define revival, and the definition of the term is the key to understanding the phenomenon.

The word for "revive" used in the prayer of Psalm 85:6 is a form of the verb *chayah*. The subject of the psalm is spiritual revival in Israel. *Chayah* comes from a root that means "life" and means "to restore life or to make alive." Its use in Scripture makes its exact meaning and its application to the spiritual life clear.

The Revival of Jacob

Chayah is first translated "revived" in Genesis 45.

> *So he [Joseph] sent his brethren away, and they departed: and he said unto them, See that ye fall not out by the way. And they went up out of Egypt, and came into the land of Canaan unto Jacob their father, and told him, saying, Joseph is yet alive, and he is governor over all the land of Egypt. And Jacob's heart fainted, for he believed them not. And they told him all the words of Joseph, which he had said unto them: and when he saw the wagons which Joseph had sent to carry him, the spirit of Jacob their father revived: And Israel said, It is enough; Joseph my son is yet alive: I will go and see him before I die* (vv. 24–28).

Of course a form of *chayah* is used in verse 27: "*And when he saw the wagons which Joseph had sent to carry him, the spirit of Jacob their father revived.*" The revival of Jacob was an emotional revival. The patriarch's mental state had been one of self-imposed depression for over twenty years, based on his belief that Joseph (his favorite son) had been killed (see Genesis 37:31–35 and also Genesis 42:36–38). When he got word and saw evidence that Joseph was "*yet alive,*" the Bible says that "*the spirit of Jacob . . . revived.*"

In this experience, Jacob's mental and emotional condition was restored to a state of health and happiness. His "revival" was a return to emotional normality.

The Revival of Samson

Chayah is next used in the Hebrew Bible when the story of Samson is told. In Judges 15, we read of Samson's physical exhaustion after his slaughter of a thousand Philistines with the jawbone of an ass.

And he was sore athirst, and called on the LORD, and said, Thou hast given this great deliverance into the hand of thy servant: and now shall I die for thirst, and fall into the hand of the uncircumcised? But God clave an hollow place that was in the jaw, and there came water thereout; and when he had drunk, his spirit came again, and he revived: wherefore he called the name thereof Enhakkore, which is in Lehi unto this day (vv. 18–19).

Of course *chayah* is used where the Bible says that "*when he had drunk* [the water] . . . *he revived.*" The drink of water restored Samson to a state of physical health and normality. His revival simply brought him back to normal.

The Revival of the Widow's Son

I Kings 17 records a miracle performed through Elijah and uses a form of *chayah.*

And he stretched himself upon the child three times, and cried unto the LORD, and said, O LORD my God, I pray thee, let this child's soul come into him again. And the LORD heard the voice of Elijah; and the soul of the child came into him again, and he revived (vv. 21–22).

The "revival" of this child was his restoration to life. Being alive is the normal state of a child, and so the reviving involved returning the boy to normal.

Revival in English

Usually the word *revive* in English is used in this same way. It comes from the Latin for "live again" and carries the idea of restoring to normal. When we say that a person needs to be "revived" physically, we mean that he is in a subnormal state of health. Perhaps he is unconscious or maybe not even breathing. Something must be done to "revive" him. By this we mean simply that we must work to restore him to a normal state of health and strength!

Reviving somebody does not mean giving him extraordinary physical powers. It does not mean invigorating him beyond the normal. It just means bringing him back to the way he should be. This is also what "revival" means in the Scriptures when applied to the spiritual life of God's people.

The Revival Psalm

Psalm 85 is clearly speaking of the spiritual life of Israel. In verses 1 through 3, David thanks the Lord that He has *"brought back"* His people from sin and disobedience in the past and restored them to the spiritual and moral level where He could bless them.

> *LORD, thou hast been favourable unto thy land: thou hast brought back the captivity of Jacob. Thou hast forgiven the iniquity of thy people, thou hast covered all their sin. Selah. Thou hast taken away all thy wrath: thou hast turned thyself from the fierceness of thine anger.*

In verses 4 through 7, David asks that God do it again. He wants the Lord to "turn" Israel back to Himself that the people might again know His forgiveness, mercy, and blessing.

> *Turn us, O God of our salvation, and cause thine anger toward us to cease. Wilt thou be angry with us for ever? Wilt thou draw out thine anger to all generations? wilt thou not revive us again: that thy people may rejoice in thee? Show us thy mercy, O LORD, and grant us thy salvation.*

In this context is the prayer that asks God to *"revive us again,"* which employs the usual Hebrew term *chayah* for quickening and restoration. It means to "bring us back to the spiritual state that should be normal for Your people."

The Longest Psalm

Psalm 119 includes a number of prayers asking God to grant the writer a spiritual revival. In this, the longest of the psalms, the Authorized English Version translates *chayah* with the word quicken. The prayers for quickening are found in verses 25, 37, 40, 50, 88, 93, 107, 149, 154, 156, and 159. One of them reads as follows: "*Quicken me after thy lovingkindness; so shall I keep the testimony of thy mouth*" (v. 88). The psalmist wants God to restore him spiritually so that he will obey His Word.

Verse 93 indicates that the Word of God is the means by which God's servants are revived as well as the standard to which they are restored. "*I will never forget thy precepts: for with them thou hast quickened me.*"

Revival by the Word is not only a moral restoration but also apparently a restoration of spiritual strength. "*I am afflicted very much: quicken me, O LORD, according unto thy word*" (v. 107; see also vv. 25, 50).

The writer of Psalm 119 repeatedly calls upon God to bring him up to the standard of Scripture. This request is not seeking something beyond what the Lord calls upon His people to experience normally. The revival of which *chayah* speaks is nothing other than a physical, emotional, or spiritual restoration to the normal.

Old Testament Revival

When one speaks of spiritual revival as a return to spiritual normality, he is using the terms in relation to the definition of the word *norm*, which means "a standard, model, or pattern." When people are revived, God brings them to a level of living that fits the scriptural standard.

For the Israelite in Old Testament days, the "norm" was to be obedient to God's Law as given to His people through Moses. Obeying the Law brought the promise of definite blessings. Remember that God told Joshua,

> *Be thou strong and very courageous, that thou mayest observe to do according to all the law, which Moses my servant commanded thee: turn not from it to the right hand or to the left, that thou mayest prosper whithersoever thou goest. This book of the law shall not depart out of thy mouth; but thou shalt meditate therein day and night, that thou*

mayest observe to do according to all that is written therein: for then thou shalt make thy way prosperous, and then thou shalt have good success (Joshua 1:7–8).

The many blessings promised to Israel in the "normal" state of obedience are listed primarily in Deuteronomy 28 and Joshua 1. The Israelites could expect victory in battle, financial prosperity, good health, growing families, and nearness to God as long as they would "*hearken diligently unto the voice of the Lord thy God, to observe and to do all his commandments*" (Deuteronomy 28:1). These blessings would disappear "*if thou wilt not hearken unto the voice of the Lord thy God*" (Deuteronomy 28:15), and certain curses would come. The prayer of Psalm 85:6 was that the Lord would restore Israel to the condition of obedience so that His people would be back in the place of blessing. This is what Old Testament revivals really were—a return to the normal with the return of the blessings. It was something Israel repeatedly experienced, and it was the goal for which God's prophets labored throughout the Old Testament age!

New Testament Revival

Although the word revive is not used in any of the New Testament books to mean what the Old Testament writers meant by it, the concept is definitely there. Jesus Christ set a definite norm for the life of the New Testament believer, and it is described repeatedly.

In Matthew: "*If any man will come after me, let him deny himself, and take up his cross, and follow me*" (16:24).

In Mark: "*Preach the gospel to every creature*" (16:15).

In Luke/Acts: "*Endued with power from on high*" (Luke 24:49).

In John: "*He that abideth in me, and I in him, the same bringeth forth much fruit: for without me ye can do nothing*" (15:5).

In Romans: "*Present your bodies a living sacrifice, holy, acceptable unto God, which is your reasonable service*" (12:1).

In the Corinthian epistles: "*That they which live should not henceforth live unto themselves, but unto him which died for them, and rose again*" (II Corinthians 5:15).

In Galatians: "*Walk in the Spirit, and ye shall not fulfil the lust of the flesh*" (5:16).

In Ephesians: "*Be filled with the Spirit*" (5:18).

In Philippians: "*Press toward the mark for the prize of the high calling of God in Christ Jesus*" (3:14).

In Colossians: "*Set your affection on things above, not on things on the earth*" (3:2).

The surrendered, Spirit-filled life is the normal life of the Christian, according to the New Testament! And Jesus taught in John 13 through 17 that this state of submission and faith should be expected to bring five definite experiences to our lives:

1. Remarkable answers to prayer (John 14:12–14; 15:16; 16:23–24)
2. Obvious help from the Holy Spirit (John 14:15–26; 15:26–27; 16:7–15)
3. Love, joy, and peace in the heart (John 14:27; 15:9–11; 16:32–33)
4. Much fruit (15:1–8)
5. Persecution (15:18–25; 16:1–4)

Each of these was experienced by the Spirit-filled believers in the Acts of the Apostles! The committed, empowered living of the early Christians was normal for New Testament believers, and the blessings Jesus promised and gave should be considered normal for us too. To have a revival in this Age of the Spirit and of the Church is to have God bring us back from carnality to spirituality, from disobedience to surrender, from love of the world to love of the Father, from malaise to health, from subnormal to normal. When we are not seeing the results of the Spirit-filled life that Jesus told us to expect, we must assume that we need a revival. And we must seek it earnestly.

James 4

Several New Testament Scriptures call for revival among worldly, carnal, and disobedient Christians. Notice Romans 13:10–14.

> *Love worketh no ill to his neighbour: therefore love is*
> *the fulfilling of the law. And that, knowing the time, that*
> *now it is high time to awake out of sleep: for now is our*
> *salvation nearer than when we believed. The night is far*
> *spent, the day is at hand: let us therefore cast off the works*
> *of darkness, and let us put on the armour of light. Let us*
> *walk honestly, as in the day; not in rioting and drunkenness,*
> *not in chambering and wantonness, not in strife and envy-*
> *ing. But put ye on the Lord Jesus Christ, and make not pro-*
> *vision for the flesh, to fulfil the lusts thereof.*

Find similar calls in Galatians 5 and in Revelation 2 and 3. The fourth chapter of James has an especially strong call for revival.

> *Draw nigh to God, and he will draw nigh to you. Cleanse*
> *your hands, ye sinners; and purify your hearts, ye double*
> *minded. Be afflicted, and mourn, and weep: let your laugh-*
> *ter be turned to mourning, and your joy to heaviness. Humble*
> *yourselves in the sight of the Lord, and he shall lift you up*
> (vv. 8–10).

The Apostle James charges the recipients of his epistle with worldliness, prayerlessness, and selfishness at the beginning of this chapter. Then he calls upon them to "*draw nigh to God*" with the promise that when they do, "*he will draw nigh to you.*" James tells them to confess their sins, to purify their hearts, and to humble themselves with tears. In response to repentance and submission, God will "*lift you up.*" This is revival. God will re-store His people to normal if they will earnestly and believingly turn to Him.

Normal

When we say that the churches need revival, we are not speaking of some exceptional blessing that the Lord might or might not wish to grant. Physical healing, material wealth, or some strong personal wish may not be in God's plan for us. We may pray for such things, but we have no assurance from the Bible that God will necessarily give them. However, blessings that the Bible reveals are according to God's will, and especially those blessings that the Lord has promised, are a different matter entirely.

> *And this is the confidence that we have in him, that, if we ask any thing according to his will, he heareth us: and if we know that he hear us, whatsoever we ask, we know that we have the petitions that we desired of him* (I John 5:14–15).

If revival is understood as an extraordinary and exceptional blessing not supported by biblical promises, then we will think of it as a sovereign act of God that cannot be sought with any real expectation. If, however, revival is understood as restoring Christians to normal, and if we find it promised in the Bible to contrite-hearted seekers, then it can be expected when we meet the conditions (see Isaiah 57:15). If the spiritual level of our churches is normal according to scriptural standards, then they do not need a revival by its biblical definition. If, however, the powerlessness and carnality prevalent in most evangelical congregations are less than New Testament normality (which of course they are), then clearly we need and must have revival! Now is not the time for Christians to give up on revival. The Bible shows us that God is the Great Reviver of His people! When they turn from their idols and their sin and turn to Him in contrite and humble faith, He will always revive them. Not finding the power within ourselves to bring our lives up to the place of blessing, we must call upon the Lord to do it for us. Every sin must be forsaken and every promise believed, but when we do, we can look expectantly for God to draw nigh to us again!

CHAPTER 2

His Soul Was Grieved

And the children of Israel cried unto the LORD, saying, We have sinned against thee, both because we have forsaken our God, and also served Baalim. And the LORD said unto the children of Israel, Did not I deliver you from the Egyptians, and from the Amorites, from the children of Ammon, and from the Philistines? The Zidonians also, and the Amalekites, and the Maonites, did oppress you; and ye cried to me, and I delivered you out of their hand. Yet ye have forsaken me, and served other gods: wherefore I will deliver you no more. Go and cry unto the gods which ye have chosen; let them deliver you in the time of your tribulation. And the children of Israel said unto the LORD, We have sinned: do thou unto us whatsoever seemeth good unto thee; deliver us only, we pray thee, this day. And they put away the strange gods from among them, and served the LORD: and his soul was grieved for the misery of Israel. (Judges 10:10–16)

Can we expect God to respond to prayer for revival? When His people repent and turn back to Him, do we have any indication in the Bible about what the Lord will do? The passage we have just read certainly says that we do!

The Book of Judges is very helpful in giving us an understanding of revival. It records the series of revivals and apostasies that occurred in Israel between the death of Joshua and the establishment of the monarchy (a period of more than 300 years). In Chapter 2, the writer summarizes the pattern that characterized that period.

> *They forsook the LORD, and served Baal and Ashtaroth. And the anger of the LORD was hot against Israel, and he delivered them into the hands of spoilers that spoiled them, and he sold them into the hands of their enemies round about, so that they could not any longer stand before their enemies. Whithersoever they went out, the hand of the LORD was against them for evil, as the LORD had said, and as the LORD had sworn unto them: and they were greatly distressed. Nevertheless the LORD raised up judges, which delivered them out of the hand of those that spoiled them. And yet they would not hearken unto their judges, but they went a whoring after other gods, and bowed themselves unto them: they turned quickly out of the way which their fathers walked in, obeying the commandments of the LORD; but they did not so. And when the LORD raised them up judges, then the LORD was with the judge, and delivered them out of the hand of their enemies all the days of the judge: for it repented the LORD because of their groanings by reason of them that oppressed them and vexed them. And it came to pass, when the judge was dead, that they returned, and corrupted themselves more than their fathers, in following other gods to serve them, and to bow down unto them; they ceased not from their own doings, nor from their stubborn way* (vv. 13–19).

There was a cycle of spiritual rises and falls throughout this time. The cycle followed this pattern:

The people would forsake the Lord and serve idols.

God would send an enemy to oppress them in order to chastise them to repentance.

The people would repent of their sins and pray for deliverance.

God would forgive them and send them a deliverer (called a "judge") to lead them in a miraculous overthrow of the enemy.

The people served God relatively well as long as that judge was living and led them; but when he died, they forsook the Lord again.

God would then send another oppressor, and the whole process was repeated.

We notice further, in Judges 2:19, that in each new apostasy, the people of Israel "*corrupted themselves more than their fathers.*" Over the long run, the pattern in Judges was not so much a cycle as it was a spiral. The revivals were relative. Israel came back to God under chastisement, but not as far back or as close to God as they had been before! In each apostasy-revival-apostasy, the nation became worse: less spiritual and more ignorant of God's truth. Any reader of Judges can see that Israel was spiraling down, and the end of the story is that "*every man did that which was right in his own eyes*" (21:25). The book thus shows us that spiritual revivals are relative in some ways. God may revive a people who are wrong theologically in some matters or wrong in their understanding of right living in some ways. Men can repent from the heart but be confused in the head and still have God's renewal!

The book also teaches that God will respond to the repentance of His people. That fact is very clearly demonstrated in Chapters 10 and 11 where the rise of the judge Jephthah to defeat the Ammonites is recorded. When "*the children of Israel did evil again in the sight of the LORD*" after the death of Gideon, "*the anger of the Lord was hot against Israel, and he sold them into the hands of the Philistines, and into the hands of the children of Ammon*" (Judges 10:6–7). These oppressors "*vexed and oppressed*" the nation for a number of years, and finally the people "*cried unto the Lord, saying, We have sinned*" (vv. 8–10).

God's reply to them is ominous but understandable. "*Go and cry unto the gods which ye have chosen; let them deliver you in the time of your tribulation*" (v. 14). He told them, "*I will deliver you no more*" (v. 13). How many times would Jehovah let His covenant people take advantage of His mercy by forsaking Him when times were good and then turning to Him when times were hard? He was justified in telling them to ask their idols for deliverance, since they called them "gods." His patience had apparently worn out, and Israel could no longer expect His help.

But the people confessed their sins anyway (v. 15). They submitted themselves to the will of the Lord and got rid of their "*strange gods*" (v. 16). They served the true God and prayed for His deliverance, even though they had no reason to expect Him to answer those prayers. Then the Bible says of the Lord that "*his soul was grieved for the misery of Israel*" (v. 16). His heart moved in compassion toward His penitent people. In the next chapter (11), God grants the deliverance for which they prayed and revives them again!

Revival in the Bible is God's bringing His people back. When man repents, God will repent. This principle can be found all throughout Scripture. When we turn from our sins, He will turn from His wrath. The revival at Nineveh is a powerful example of this. When the prophet Jonah entered that sinful city, his message was of divine judgment with no hint of mercy. "*Yet forty days, and Nineveh shall be overthrown*" (Jonah 3:4). The preacher's manner was without compassion, as we learn from Jonah 4, but nevertheless the people of the city were moved to repent. "*So the people of Nineveh believed God, and proclaimed a fast*" (Jonah 3:5). Everyone from the king to the beggar turned from his sins and prayed to Jonah's God. "*Who can tell,*" said the king, "*if God will turn and repent, and turn away his fierce anger, that we perish not?*" (Jonah 3:6–10). God did repent, canceling His order for Nineveh's destruction. When people turn, God turns. That is the basic rule for revival!

See it in Psalm 80.

> *Turn us again, O God, and cause thy face to shine; and we shall be saved* (vv. 3, 7, and 19).

Find it in the first chapter of Zechariah's prophecy.

> *Turn ye unto me, saith the LORD of hosts, and I will turn unto you, saith the LORD of hosts* (v. 3).

In the New Testament, it is clearly presented in James 4:8–10.

> *Draw nigh to God, and he will draw nigh to you. Cleanse your hands, ye sinners; and purify your hearts, ye double minded. Be afflicted, and mourn, and weep: let your laughter be turned to mourning, and your joy to heaviness. Humble yourselves in the sight of the Lord, and he shall lift you up.*

Is God in any sense predictable? He is, according to the Bible, when His essential nature and eternal promises call for a certain response. God can be expected to revive His people when they repent of their sins and call upon Him. When Israel turned to the Lord, "*His soul [nephesh–God's very life] was grieved.*" The nature of the true God caused Him to show mercy and revive His people! There are many strange ideas about revival today, some of the worst of which deny the principle that God responds to repentance.

Some teach that revival is a "sovereign act of God," unpredictable and unrelated to human actions or prayers. Certainly God is sovereign; He rules the universe according to the good pleasure of His will. Yet the idea that revival is a sovereign act falsely indicates that God revives people independently, without regard to their words or attitudes. To be a sovereign act, revival must not be conditioned on man's repentance or submission. This idea contradicts a great amount of preaching over the years which has taught that God revives people in response to their meeting His conditions. II Chronicles 7:14 shows that God was predictable in regard to revival in Israel. Although He is sovereign, He does not send revival as a sovereign act, but rather as a promised response! The Bible teaches that when men respond to God's call, He responds to their response. This is why we can expect revival when we meet the conditions.

Some teach that revival is an unusual work of God, "extraordinary" and beyond what can be considered "normal." This idea demonstrates how confused Christians have become about revival! The words *revive, revived,* or *reviving* appear a total of fourteen times in the Authorized English Old Testament, each time translated from a form of the Hebrew word *chayah.* This same Hebrew word is rendered *quicken* fourteen times in the Book of Psalms with the same meaning as "revive." It is a verb conveying the idea of life or living. Some forms mean to live and others mean to cause to live. It can have the meaning of keeping alive, letting live, or restoring to life. Even in English, to revive means to restore to a normal state of health and life. When a medical technician works to "revive" somebody, he is not trying to energize him to an extraordinary, supernormal state of health or strength. He will use CPR to bring him back to normal. People who need physical revival are physically sick. The need for spiritual revival presupposes spiritual sickness. When God revives His people, He brings them from spiritual illness to spiritual health, from disobedience to obedience, from carnality to spirituality, from rebellion to surrender.

In Old Testament days, the Lord promised His people certain blessings if they would obey the commandments He gave them through Moses. Disobedience to the commandments would reverse God's attitude and turn the blessings into curses (read all of Deuteronomy 28). Revival for Israel would have meant the nation coming back to the "norm" of obedience to the Lord's law and to the expected bestowal of these blessings.

In the New Testament age, God has promised definite blessings to Christians who live by faith in Christ and in obedience to His commands. The thirteenth through the seventeenth chapters of the Book of John record a talk Jesus had with His disciples the night before He was crucified. In it He described what they could expect in the time of His absence. "*I go away, and come again unto you,*" He said (14:28). The period between His ascension into Heaven and His return from Heaven has been called the Church Age. It might also be called the Age of the Holy Spirit, because the Lord said that the most important aspect of this time would be the presence of God's Spirit within the bodies of believers!

If ye love me, keep my commandments. And I will pray the Father, and he shall give you another Comforter, that he may abide with you for ever; even the Spirit of truth; whom the world cannot receive, because it seeth him not, neither knoweth him: but ye know him; for he dwelleth with you, and shall be in you (14:15–17).

Because "the Spirit of truth" lives within us, we can expect five powerful experiences to characterize our lives: direct answers to prayer (14:12–14; 15:7, 16; 16:23–27), obvious help from the Holy Spirit (14:15–26; 15:26–27; 16:7–14), peace and joy all the time (14:27–28; 15:9–11; 16:33), much fruit (15:1–16), and persecution (15:17–16:6).

These experiences will come upon believers who live in submission to God. We certainly find them all recorded in the Book of Acts when the Christians were living right. The term "filled with the Spirit" describes the normal state of believers in the New Testament age. When we are not Spirit-filled, we are in need of a revival. A revival for Christians involves coming back to the normal Christian life with the expected blessings of John 13–17. When these blessings are absent, we are in need of a revival!

A great man once said that most Christians are so subnormal that when some rise to the normal, they are considered supernormal! Here is the problem we face. Worldliness, carnality, and indifference have become so much the usual condition of Christians that passion, power, and purity seem extraordinary! Let us recognize that Bible Christianity is a very powerful thing whenever and wherever it is lived out. Sadly, we have so seldom seen it that men are persuaded that it is beyond the normal. Yet if the New Testament gives us the standard, then prevailing prayer, effective evangelism, abiding peace, Spirit enablement, as well as severe persecution are the norm for the Christian life. Our unbiblical conception of revival points to our great need for it!

A third strange and incorrect idea that we often hear is that revival must meet certain historical criteria to be correctly called "revival." It is amazing how unscriptural are the requirements some believers set for revival! The number of conversions, the endurance of the converts, the effects on society, and unusual phenomena are all considered when critics decide whether or not a religious occurrence is a "revival." But a revival is not in closed taverns, reduced crime, strange experiences, massive numbers, or church harmony. It is in believers turning back to a life surrendered to God! When God revives His people, their witness for Christ has new power, but the specific effects of that power may not match exactly the effects of other revivals in the past.

The second chapter of Acts says that Peter and the congregation at Jerusalem were "*filled with the Holy Ghost*" (v. 4) and spoke the Word of God in His power. They were in a state of revival. As a result, those who heard their witness to the resurrection of Christ "*were pricked in their heart*" (v. 37) and repented. Some three thousand were saved and baptized as a result of the revival on that Day of Pentecost (v. 41).

The seventh chapter of Acts tells about the deacon Stephen, who was "*full of the Holy Ghost*" (v. 55). He was in a state of revival, and as he witnessed for Christ before the council of men that had arranged for the Lord's crucifixion, the power of God brought conviction. "*They were cut to the heart,*" the Bible says (v. 54), but the result was rage, not conversion. These sinful men "*ran upon him* [Stephen] . . . *and cast him out of the city*" (vv. 57–58). There they stoned the deacon to death. But let us note that there was a state of revival in the Christian of Acts 7 just as surely as there was such a state among the Christians in Acts 2! The revival was in the hearts of the believers, and the expected blessing of convicting power did come in both cases. Yet in one situation, a multitude was immediately converted, and in the other, the believer was murdered (although fruit was indeed produced through the eventual conversion of Saul—Acts 7:58 and 9:3–6). The particulars were different because they were incidentals, not essentials. Essentially, revival was the same in Acts 2 and 7. In the Bible we are instructed accurately about revival, but that is not always so in history books!

Revival is God's bringing us back to normal! Mr. Finney said, "[A revival] is the renewal of the first love of Christians, resulting in the awakening and conversion of sinners to God."[1] Bill Rice III says that revival is a return to Bible principle. Vance Havner defined revival as Christians returning to normal.

Revival is also predictable. It can be expected when it is sought on the basis of God's Word. Judges 10 shows us that we can expect revival in response to our repentance because of the very nature of the heart of God! "*His soul was grieved for the misery of Israel.*" Something in God moves when men move toward Him.

The aspect of God's nature that responds to man's repentance is His mercy. The great revival psalm, number 85, says in verse 7, "*Show us thy mercy, O LORD, and grant us thy salvation.*"

Psalm 89 says in verse 1, "*I will sing of the mercies of the LORD for ever.*"

In Psalms 106, 107, 118, and twenty-six times in Psalm 136, we read that "*his mercy endureth for ever.*" The reason God's mercy endures forever is that the eternal God is essentially merciful.

The prophet Habakkuk prayed for revival, and in his prayer he said, "*In wrath remember mercy*" (Habakkuk 3:2). God always remembers mercy in times of His wrath. Think of the covering coats He provided for Adam's nakedness on the day of his fall and God's curse. Think of Noah's ark at the time of God's terrible judgment in the Flood. God is always merciful even when He is angry, and that is because He is unalterably merciful.

Have you noticed what God did when weak and wicked King Ahab repented?

> *And the word of the LORD came to Elijah the Tishbite, saying, Seest thou how Ahab humbleth himself before me? because he humbleth himself before me, I will not bring the evil in his days: but in his son's days will I bring the evil upon his house* (I Kings 21:28–29).

Even Ahab found God merciful, and he was the worst of the kings of Israel! Can you remember who was the most wicked ruler of the southern kingdom of Judah? It was Manasseh. Have you heard that Manasseh found God's mercy too?

> *And when he was in affliction, he besought the LORD his God, and humbled himself greatly before the God of his fathers, And prayed unto him: and he was entreated of him, and heard his supplication, and brought him again to Jerusalem into his kingdom. Then Manasseh knew that the LORD he was God* (II Chronicles 33:12–13).

The verses that follow these remarkable two tell us that the king experienced a full-scale revival in his own life and spent the rest of his days working to undo the harm he had done by his sins! How could such a man have a revival? The answer is in the fact that God is and will always be merciful and that His reviving work can be expected in response to our repentance. Hear what God's messengers have told us!

> *In the time of their trouble, when they cried unto thee, thou heardest them from heaven; and according to thy manifold mercies thou gavest them saviours* (Nehemiah 9:27).

> *Thus saith the high and lofty One that inhabiteth eternity, whose name is Holy; I dwell in the high and holy place, with him also that is of a contrite and humble spirit, to revive the spirit of the humble, and to revive the heart of the contrite ones* (Isaiah 57:15).

> *Humble yourselves in the sight of the Lord, and he shall lift you up* (James 4:10).

Yes, we can have forgiveness, help, and blessing from God in response to humble submission, steadfast faith, sincere repentance, and solemn commitment. God is, and has always been, the Great Reviver of His people!

Certainly in our day we ought to seek personal, corporate, and general revival in the way the Israelites did in Jephthah's time. Pay attention to what characterized their quest for revival.

There Was Confession!

> *And the children of Israel said unto the LORD, We have sinned* (Judges 10:15a).

They harbored little hope for a response, but they nevertheless confessed their sins to God. Can we expect a particular reaction from God when we sincerely confess our sins?

> *If we confess our sins, he is faithful and just to forgive us our sins, and to cleanse us from all unrighteousness* (I John 1:9).

God is "faithful" to forgive when we confess. Forgiveness is not a sovereign act unrelated to our attitude, but the promised response to our confession, rooted in divine mercy.

These days, Christians who have lived their lives in love with the world and in neglect of their Father's commands ought to make serious business of confessing their sins. Godly men and women of the past have sought revival by writing out their sins and spending time confessing them. Thoughtful reflection on our sins of omission as well as our habitual sins of commission will reveal clearly why we see so little of God's blessing in our lives. However, earnest confession of all these sins will certainly secure our God's forgiveness. And the God of Israel will revive us again!

There Was Submission!

> *Do thou unto us whatsoever seemeth good unto thee* (Judges 10:15b).

The children of Israel were resigned to accept God's will for them, no matter what it was. Can we expect the Lord to do anything in particular when we yield to Him in this way? Remember Romans 12:1–2.

> *I beseech you therefore, brethren, by the mercies of God, that ye present your bodies a living sacrifice, holy, acceptable unto God, which is your reasonable service. And be not*

*conformed to this world: but be ye transformed by the re-
newing of your mind, that ye may prove what is that good,
and acceptable, and perfect, will of God.*

The admonition to surrender is attached to the promise that
those who surrender all will "prove" the perfect will of God in
their lives. The Lord will set our steps on the right path when we
submit our lives unconditionally to Him! He wants us to fulfill
His will, and He will see that we do when we become willing.
His mercy guarantees it.

There Was Prayer!

Deliver us only, we pray thee, this day (Judges 10:15c).

God gave the Israelites no words of hope that He would
answer such a prayer, but they prayed anyway. It is always right
to pray. God is "*a Rewarder of them that diligently seek him*" (Hebrews 11:6). Jesus taught us to expect a response to prayer.

*Ask, and it shall be given you; seek, and ye shall find;
knock, and it shall be opened unto you* (Matthew 7:7).

When we ask "*any thing according to his will,*" the Apostle John
told us, "*he heareth us*" and "*we have the petitions that we desired of
him*" (I John 5:14–15). Men who pray for things that God says He
wants for them can expect to receive the blessings they seek.

*Blessed are they which do hunger and thirst after right-
eousness: for they shall be filled* (Matthew 5:6).

Do we want revival blessings? Then we should ask for them.
Do we desire holiness? Let us ask for it. Do we hope to win
others to Christ? Let us pray that the Lord will grant these things.
It is in His nature to respond to such prayers.

There Was Repentance!

*They put away the strange gods from among them, and
served the LORD* (Judges 10:16a).

God did not tell His people that if they got rid of their idols, He would deliver them from the Ammonites. He did not lead them to believe that if they served Him again, He would come to their aid. They just did it anyway. They repented of their sins, repaired their ways, and returned to the service of the true God because it was right to do so!

And his soul was grieved.

Their repentance brought His mercy, a response we should expect.

In his journal, Benjamin Franklin described what was happening in Philadelphia as a result of George Whitefield's revival preaching. "From being thoughtless or indifferent about religion, it seem'd as if all the world were growing religious, so that one could not walk thro' the town in an evening without hearing psalms sung in different families of every street."[2]

A general revival was prevailing in the city, and it was seen and heard in the changed lives of sinner and saint alike. Sometimes I think that if Christians began to act as if a general revival had come, perhaps the Lord would send one! Perhaps we should just change our ways and see what happens! We could gather our families nightly to sing the praises of the Lord. We could start praying as if we believed that God would revive us again. We could give up the things in our lives that generate or fan the love of the world. We could begin witnessing for Christ boldly and habitually. We could have meetings to seek revival, as in times of old. Repentance turns the heart of God. Certainly we ought to repent! We can have the revival we need, as individual Christians, as servants of the Lord, and as congregations of believers. God is the Great Reviver of His people and can be expected to respond to our repentance and prayer. He is ever merciful and will hear our cry!

NOTES

[1]Charles G. Finney, *Lectures on Revivals of Religion* (New York: Fleming H. Revell Company, 1868), p. 14.

[2]Benjamin Franklin, *The Autobiography of Benjamin Franklin* (New York: Washington Square Press, 1955), pp. 128-29.

CHAPTER 3

Ideas That Hinder

Ye did run well; who did hinder you that ye should not obey the truth? This persuasion cometh not of him that calleth you. A little leaven leaveneth the whole lump. I have confidence in you through the Lord, that ye will be none otherwise minded: but he that troubleth you shall bear his judgment, whosoever he be. (Galatians 5:7–10)

Somebody was hindering spiritual progress in the "churches of Galatia," and the Apostle Paul was deeply concerned about these hindrances. By God's Spirit he wrote the Epistle to the Galatians to move them out of the way. How were these Christians being hindered? This section of Scripture reveals that wrong ideas were the hindering factors. Ideas are some of the most powerful things in the world! Wrong ideas impoverish India, enslave the Arabs, and devastate societies ruled by the Communists. Wrong ideas also hinder Fundamentalists from experiencing revival! The Northfield Conferences led by D. L. Moody and the Sword Conferences led by John R. Rice were organized to dispel wrong ideas and to expound right ideas about God's plan for the revival of His people. These and other similar conferences have done great good and have fostered spiritual awakenings across the nation and around the world. Bible truth is the basis of biblical revival, and false doctrines are obstacles to it. In the Book of Galatians we find refuted several serious fallacies that still hinder people today.

Galatians is a beautiful treatise on the way to spiritual "liberty" (2:4; 4:26; 5:1, 13). Throughout the epistle we learn this truth: *Grace by faith in the Spirit produces liberty. This plan is opposed to the formula of Law by works in the flesh, which results in bondage.* These opposing formulas are contrasted throughout the book. They are applied both to salvation and sanctification. Grace-Faith-Spirit is the right idea, and Law-Works-Flesh is the wrong one. This contrast has definite applications to the issues of revival, and several of them enlighten us in regard to the ideas that are hindering revival among Fundamentalists. Here are four bad ideas that are common in our day.

1. Let's Define Revival from History

Essential to a productive discussion of revival is a correct understanding of what revival is. Only the Bible can give us the right answers to our questions, and manmade messages can only hinder our pursuit of revival. See what Paul said in Galatians 1 about the message he preached.

> *Paul, an apostle, (not of men, neither by man, but by Jesus Christ . . .) (v. 1).*

> *But though we, or an angel from heaven, preach any other gospel unto you than that which we have preached unto you, let him be accursed (v. 8).*

> *But I certify you, brethren, that the gospel which was preached of me is not after man. For I neither received it of man, neither was I taught it, but by the revelation of Jesus Christ (vv. 11–12).*

Ideas of human origin cannot shed light on spiritual problems. We must look to divine revelation, to Holy Scripture, for the definition of revival and for directions in obtaining it!

A strange phenomenon in our day is the frequency with which men who denounce experience as a source of doctrine will admit to being influenced by experience in their own interpretation of Christian doctrine! To define revival, they look to history and insist on the interpretation some have given to their experiences with revival as the basis of their definition. As we have seen, the biblical concept of revival is God's bringing His people back to the "normal" state of obedience and blessing. However, many today insist that revival is an extraordinary event produced by a sovereign act of God. They look back through history and see the Great Awakening as a powerful surprise and the Second Great Awakening as an unfortunate mixture of good and bad. They declare that the evangelistic efforts of Calvinists such as Asahel Nettleton and the Prayer Revival of the late 1850s were good, but that the preaching campaigns of Charles Finney and his like were harmful counterfeits. They affirm that no human preparation or prayer preceded the Great Awakening and that no lasting good resulted from Finney's ministry, even though historical facts contradict both assertions! They want history to prove that real revival comes without men seeking it. But we should never rely on anyone's record or interpretation of man's experience to define the doctrine of revival. We must find that in the Bible!

> *Wilt thou be angry with us for ever? wilt thou draw out thine anger to all generations? Wilt thou not revive us again: that thy people may rejoice in thee? Shew us thy mercy, O LORD, and grant us thy salvation* (Psalm 85:5–7).

Recently an old friend of mine published an account of why he had adopted a strict Calvinistic theology that changed his approach to revival and evangelism. To my amazement, he credited some most unworthy factors with producing his theological conversion. First, he said it was pragmatism. Now he did not use that word, but that was exactly what he was saying! When in the past he had followed an aggressive evangelistic approach and believed in revivalism, he was disappointed with the results. It didn't work. But do we change our doctrine when we don't see results? Does Scripture change because our attempts at applying its teachings disappoint us? Will our theology be dictated by the Bible or by pragmatism?

Secondly, he said experience had changed his mind. He can tell you about the bad things he discovered among the non-Calvinists he had admired. Sadly, many who once believed in seeking revival have been hindered by things that have happened or not happened. But doctrine ought not to come from experience!

Thirdly, he credited reading with persuading him in a new direction. He read the best Calvinistic books and was convinced. He read some weak critiques of strict Calvinism and concluded that there must not be any good arguments on the other side. However, truth must be determined from God's Book, not man's books, whether convincing or disappointing. We are hindered when we are caught in the web of manmade ideas. We must look to the Bible to define revival and to find the way to revival! Let us reject the idea of self-inspiration—man's devising doctrine from his own mind and experience.

2. Let's Improve the Plan of Salvation

Now nobody puts it that way, but for some time certain Fundamentalists have bewailed the way evangelists present the gospel and have called for an improvement. The improvements they propose always involve including works in some subtle way. Without intending to do so, these teachers advocate swerving from the Grace-Faith-Spirit formula to the Law-Works-Flesh delusion. In Galatians 2, Paul replies to such propositions.

> *False brethren . . . came in privily to spy out our liberty which we have in Christ Jesus, that they might bring us into bondage: to whom we gave place by subjection, no, not for an hour; that the truth of the gospel might continue with you* (vv. 4–5).

> *I do not frustrate the grace of God: for if righteousness come by the law, then Christ is dead in vain* (v. 21).

In verses 15 through 20, we are told that sinners, Jew or Gentile, are "*not justified by the works of the law, but by the faith of Jesus Christ.*" Simple trust in Christ and His redeeming blood brings eternal salvation. However, some of the Jewish-Christian teachers from Jerusalem were concerned that Paul's gospel was not adequate. Certainly we should expect something more from his so-called Gentile converts than simply a profession of faith. A true believer in the Jewish Messiah would accept the Abrahamic Covenant, be circumcised, and follow the Law of Moses as good Jews always have, wouldn't he? A real "convert" will join God's chosen people, won't he?

Some today will also make much of what should be expected of a new convert to Christ. If they don't see what they want to see, they will re-examine what the individual did to be saved. Too often in all of this examination, they put works into the plan of salvation and ruin the Grace-Faith-Spirit formula.

Everybody ought to believe that repentance is required for salvation because the Bible says so.

> *I came not to call the righteous, but sinners to repentance* (Luke 5:32).

> *Likewise, I say unto you, there is joy in the presence of the angels of God over one sinner that repenteth* (Luke 15:10).

> *The Lord is not slack concerning his promise, as some men count slackness; but is longsuffering to us-ward, not willing that any should perish, but that all should come to repentance* (II Peter 3:9).

Repentance for salvation is right, but commitment to do something proven by the doing of it is not the repentance that saves. It is works for salvation.

The Greek word for *repent* in the New Testament means "to change one's mind." The Bible is clear that men are saved by faith in Christ, but it is also clear that the faith that brings salvation requires a change of mind. The sinner changes his mind in order to believe in Christ. About what must we change our minds in order to trust Jesus for salvation? Mark 1:4 indicates that we must repent of sin. Mark 1:15 directs us to repent of our unbelief ("*repent ye, and believe the gospel*"—change your mind and believe!). Philippians 3:1–9 and Hebrews 6:1 call upon sinners to repent of their good works (as the object of their dependence for salvation). In order to be saved, a man must change his mind about sin, about faith in Jesus Christ, and about his own good works. Saving faith is full dependence on Jesus alone for redemption, justification, and eternal life! It is not just the acceptance of orthodox doctrine, or the addition of a belief to one's creed, or the praying of a certain prayer. It requires a definite decision, a change of mind, repentance!

But repentance is not a promise to do better, and doing better is not the required test of saving repentance. If this were the definition of repentance in salvation, then true salvation would require three steps: repentance (commitment to obey), faith (trust for power to obey), and performance (actual obedience). No matter how you look at that, it puts works into the plan of salvation. This new plan does not improve the plan of salvation by grace; it ruins it.

Yes, repentance is required for salvation, but we must not misdefine it. And regeneration is the result of salvation, but we must not claim the ability to discern it every time. The statement that "*ye shall know them by their fruits*" is in the chapter (Matthew 7) that begins with Jesus saying, "*Judge not, that ye be not judged.*" The inspection of fruit is about detecting "*false prophets*" (v. 15) and not about judging people's salvation.

Misguided attempts to improve on salvation-by-grace preaching usually confuse Bible teaching about discipleship with the teaching about salvation. Both doctrines are important, but they deal with different issues. The Lord Jesus called men to salvation with the invitation, "*Come unto me*" (Matthew 11:28). He called men to discipleship with the invitation, "*Come after me*" (Matthew 16:24). In the Book of John, a clear distinction is made between believers in Jesus Christ and disciples of Jesus. See this in John 2:11, where His disciples became believers ("*and his disciples believed on him*"). See the distinction in John 6:60–66, where many disciples were exposed as unbelievers ("*there are some of you that believe not*"). See it again in John 8:30–31, where believers were urged to become disciples ("*Then said Jesus to those Jews which believed on him, If ye continue in my word, then are ye my disciples indeed*").

The New Testament does make discipleship distinct from salvation, and the differences are many. Salvation is secured by simple faith in Christ (John 6:47); discipleship is achieved by commitment to obey Christ (Matthew 16:24). In salvation, one receives a gift ("*eternal life*," Romans 6:23); in discipleship, one gives a gift ("*your bodies*," Romans 12:1). The salvation decision must be made only once, since the results depend entirely on Christ (John 4:13–14); the discipleship decision must be repeated regularly because the results depend somewhat on us (Luke 9:23). Salvation cannot fail (John 10:28); discipleship is always in danger of failing (Luke 14:25–33). Salvation will bring eternal life (John 3:16); successful discipleship will bring eternal rewards (Matthew 16:27). They are related and vitally important, but salvation and discipleship are different. To mix and mingle the requirements of each is to pervert the gospel and to preach a message of good works for everlasting life! Although the proponents would never admit it, the Lordship-Salvation doctrine is but another form of self-salvation, and it is wrong.

3. Let's Not Talk Too Much about the Holy Spirit

The third chapter of Galatians opens with a series of questions. Notice the two in verses 2 and 3. "*Received ye the Spirit by the works of the law, or by the hearing of faith? Are ye so foolish? having begun in the Spirit, are ye now made perfect by the flesh?*"

With these questions, Paul begins to explain that the contrast between Law-Works-Flesh and Grace-Faith-Spirit is not only involved in the matter of salvation but also in sanctification. Just as men are saved by God's grace through faith in Christ by the power of the Spirit, so also Christians are sanctified (made holy in their lives) by the same formula. The Bible teaches us that the sanctification of believers in their daily lives is a gradual process, not an instant transformation (see I Thessalonians 4:1). But it is not an automatic process. Our growth in holiness comes only by the Holy Spirit through faith in Christ. Yet many Christians seem to think that we are to trust Christ for salvation and then try hard for victory over sin! As a result they are regularly frustrated and defeated. The key to power for victory and service is the presence and power of the Spirit in the lives of believers, accessed by faith. "*This I say then, Walk in the Spirit, and ye shall not fulfil the lust of the flesh*" (Galatians 5:16).

This is why Fundamentalists must start talking again about the Holy Spirit! Ephesians 1 says that Christians were immediately and permanently sealed with the Spirit when they believed on the Lord Jesus (see vv. 12–14). The fifth chapter of the same epistle says that those who have been sealed with the Spirit have a duty to be filled with the Spirit (v. 18). To have the Holy Spirit directing and empowering our life and work is the very essence of true Christian living. How can we excuse neglecting this teaching?

In the great nineteenth-century revivals, the fullness of the Spirit was often discussed and widely experienced. In time, revived believers differed in the particulars of this doctrine. Holiness men such as Morrison and Warner saw sinless perfection as the purpose of the Spirit's ministry in the Christian. Evangelists such as Moody and Torrey saw power in proclaiming the gospel as the primary purpose of the ministry of the Spirit, although they also taught the necessity of the Spirit's involvement in victory over the flesh. Those influenced by the Plymouth Brethren, such as those who led the early Bible conference and Bible institute movements, taught a theology that de-emphasized experience with the Holy Spirit. They saw Pentecost as merely a dispensational transition and being filled with the Spirit as basically synonymous with ordinary obedience. With the rise of Pentecostalism out of the Holiness movement and its proliferation through the Charismatic movement, biblical Fundamentalists reacted against the extremes of the tongues-speakers by retreating from the Moody/Torrey position so generally held by their kind in the early days into the Bible institute position. Gradually, preaching on the ministry of the Spirit has diminished in Fundamentalist churches, and the effect has been devastating. The deadness of the flesh pervades many orthodox and technically separated churches. Without knowing it, many good people have swallowed the miserable idea of self-sanctification and lost sight of God's Spirit. Oh for a renewal of sound preaching on the Spirit in Fundamentalist circles today!

4. Let's Get in Touch with This New Generation

The Judaizers that Paul opposed in his epistle to the Galatians had found a combination that attracts preachers and church people yet in our day! They thought they had found a way to preach the gospel without suffering because of its offensive nature. Paul wrote, "*If I yet preach circumcision, why do I yet suffer persecution? then is the offence of the cross ceased*" (Galatians 5:11).

Those who preached "circumcision" were avoiding a serious problem. The first Christians were Jews who saw in Jesus both their Messiah and their Savior. When Paul and other missionary evangelists took the gospel of Christ to the pagans of Gentile lands, they were sorely criticized and persecuted by their Jewish kinsmen. As great numbers of uncircumcised Gentiles who did not observe the rituals and rules of the Mosaic Law were accepted into Christian congregations, unbelieving Jews became more antagonistic toward the message of Jesus than ever. Families were split, and trouble mounted for the Jews who had trusted Christ. Then some teachers from the Jerusalem church invented an attractive revision of the gospel that would diffuse the situation.

Acts 15 records the Judaized gospel this way (v. 1): "*Except ye be circumcised after the manner of Moses, ye cannot be saved.*" Of the Gentiles that came to Christ, the Judaizers said, "*That it was needful to circumcise them, and to command them to keep the law of Moses*" (v. 5).

If the gospel were to be preached this way, the winning of souls to Christ would also be the winning of Gentiles to Judaism! Instead of being offensive to their Jewish kindred, evangelistic Christians would be heroes! But Paul warned his Gentile converts against the Judaized gospel.

> *As many as desire to make a fair shew in the flesh, they constrain you to be circumcised; only lest they should suffer persecution for the cross of Christ. For neither they themselves who are circumcised keep the law; but desire to have you circumcised, that they may glory in your flesh. But God forbid that I should glory, save in the cross of our Lord Jesus Christ, by whom the world is crucified unto me, and I unto the world* (Galatians 6:12–14).

After the Second World War, some well-meaning evangelistic organizations began to insist that Christians take a new approach in reaching people for the Lord, especially in reaching the young. The trappings and traditions of old-time revivalism were offensive to the current crop of Americans and had become obstacles to winning them to Christ. Evangelism must now take its cues from secular entertainment and modern advertising in order to be effective. Negatives must be replaced by positives. Preaching must not be preachy. One movement announced this slogan as its motto: "Geared to the Times; Anchored to the Rock." Although undue attachment to old-fashioned ways should not drag believers down, they must always be careful about being "geared to the times." We can see today where this approach has taken evangelicalism over time. Church music is modeled after the world (contrary to the command "*be not conformed to this world*" [Romans 12:2]). The preaching takes its style and even its subjects from the secular world. The "be-like-them-to-win-them" philosophy has made many churches not only worldly but also carnal, and although church attendance may be up, spiritual power is down!

Looking at the changes in the churches over the past fifty years would make anybody wonder who is winning whom to what. Is the church winning the world to Christ, or has the world won the church to its ways?

The issue of how a revived church will do the work of evangelism is stated very clearly in Galatians 1:10. "*For do I now persuade men, or God? or do I seek to please men? for if I yet pleased men, I should not be the servant of Christ.*"

It is a strange question that Paul asks about preaching—"Do I . . . persuade men, or God?"—and it means exactly what it says! The Greek word translated "persuade" here is used with the same meaning in Matthew 27:20, Luke 16:31, Acts 26:28, Romans 14:14, II Corinthians 5:11, Hebrews 11:13, and in many other New Testament passages. It is *peitho*, and the lexicons say it means "to convince or pacify." It refers to convincing or pleasing persuasion. The question is whether the key to effective evangelism is in pleasing and persuading people or in pleasing and persuading God. The right answer is that God must be persuaded if men are to be saved. Remember that the new birth is a miracle and that only God can do miracles. Men are "*dead in trespasses and sins*" (Ephesians 2:1–7). It would be futile to try to please or persuade a corpse to come back to life. A resurrection requires divine intervention, and the salvation of a sinner is truly bringing the dead to life ("*And you hath he quickened, who were dead*").

Christians are to seek God in order to see revival. We must please Him in order to have His power in our witness. We are to persuade Him by humbling ourselves in repentance, prayer, and faith in order to have His blessing in our attempts at evangelism. Shall we persuade God or men in order to win people to Christ? The truth is that we must "persuade . . . God." Reaching this generation is not about self-promotion but rather about divine enduement. The error of present-day evangelicalism is persuading men by pleasing them in order to win them. The need of the hour is a return to the separation of former days and more importantly to the motivation for that separation. We turn away from the world in order to please and persuade God. This is also why we pray for revival—in order to persuade God! We separate from sin and pray to the Lord in order to pave the way for revival. And we can have revival today if we will not be hindered by false ideas.

Certainly God will revive His people again if they will seek His face, conform to His will, and believe His promises. In order to follow this path, we must discard the unscriptural ideas that have hindered us (self-inspiration, self-salvation, self-sanctification, and self-promotion). To see revival we must cease looking to ourselves (our ideas, our works, our flesh, or our methods) and begin looking to God, because in Him we will find all we need to renew and empower our lives and our service.

CHAPTER 4

Not the Speech . . . But the Power

Now some are puffed up, as though I would not come to you. But I will come to you shortly, if the Lord will, and will know, not the speech of them which are puffed up, but the power. For the kingdom of God is not in word, but in power. What will ye? shall I come unto you with a rod, or in love, and in the spirit of meekness? (I Corinthians 4:18–21)

As he comes to the subject of discipline in the church, Paul refers in I Corinthians 4 to his "rod" (v. 21). "*What will ye? shall I come unto you with a rod, or in love, and in the spirit of meekness?*" What about this? What can be meant by an apostle's chastening rod? In the closing chapter of his second epistle to the church at Corinth, the Apostle Paul again seems to threaten them with a thrashing.

> *Therefore I write these things being absent, lest being present I should use sharpness, according to the power which the Lord hath given me to edification, and not to destruction* (II Corinthians 13:10).

God had given Paul "power" for their edification, but it could also be used for their "destruction." In this verse the word for power means "authority," according to the original Greek. Apostolic authority included the right to chastise in some terrible way. Hear what Paul says in II Corinthians 10.

> *Now I Paul myself beseech you by the meekness and gentleness of Christ, who in presence am base among you, but being absent am bold toward you: But I beseech you, that I may not be bold when I am present with that confidence, wherewith I think to be bold against some, which think of us as if we walked according to the flesh. For though we walk in the flesh, we do not war after the flesh . . . For though I should boast somewhat more of our authority, which the Lord hath given us for edification, and not for your destruction, I should not be ashamed: That I may not seem as if I would terrify you by letters. For his letters, say they, are weighty and powerful; but his bodily presence is weak, and his speech contemptible. Let such an one think this, that, such as we are in word by letters when we are absent, such will we be also in deed when we are present* (vv. 1–3, 8–11).

Students of the Corinthian epistles will notice repeated references to God's chastisement of disobedient believers. They even speak of such rebels suffering premature death! Paul's authority as an apostle seems to have been involved in some of this chastisement.

> *For I verily, as absent in body, but present in spirit, have judged already, as though I were present, concerning him that hath so done this deed, In the name of our Lord Jesus Christ, when ye are gathered together, and my spirit, with the power of our Lord Jesus Christ, To deliver such an one unto Satan for the destruction of the flesh, that the spirit may be saved in the day of the Lord Jesus* (I Corinthians 5:3–5).

Without question, Paul's rod was a manifestation of the power of God on his life. He spoke of this power when he reminded them of his evangelistic ministry among them.

And my speech and my preaching was not with enticing words of man's wisdom, but in demonstration of the Spirit and of power: That your faith should not stand in the wisdom of men, but in the power of God (I Corinthians 2:4–5).

Paul's challenge to his critics at Corinth was that they display "not the speech" of their position "but the power." Paul could show them the power of his teaching as well as the words.

For the kingdom of God is not in word, but in power. What will ye? shall I come unto you with a rod, or in love, and in the spirit of meekness? (I Corinthians 4:20–21).

That the Apostle Paul had critics in the Corinthian church is obvious in the epistles he wrote them. The congregation had cliques that took sides against him (see Chapter 3). Some argued against the standards of life he taught. Some opposed the doctrines he expounded. So now he calls upon them (please excuse the expression) to put up or shut up! There is power behind truth. If a proposition works, that does not necessarily prove that it is true; but if it is true, it will work! Let us not call this defense "pragmatism," since it is given by divine inspiration. There is validity to the argument that teaching may be expected to come with some experimental support. Paul's words were backed up by power. Would his critics' be? This is a good question for all of us too. In the discussion of revival issues, are our views expressed only in speech, or are they supported by power? If we say that we can pray for revival and have it, does our experience show that this is true? The Christian public will eventually want to know, "not the speech of them which are puffed up, but the power"! If we say that the harvest is plenteous and souls can be won even in hard circumstances, are we seeing souls won to demonstrate the validity of our sayings? Truth does not depend on experimental proof, but dynamic confirmation does support the truth in the minds of men.

Preachers and teachers have argued about evangelistic methods. Will "friendship evangelism" reach the multitudes, or is old-fashioned confrontation more effective? Shall area-wide revival campaigns be re-instituted, or should aggressive efforts be abandoned for innovative church programs? The fact is that books and conferences can convince some, but powerful success in reaching men will attract the attention of everyone! Evangelism that converts sinners to a new life and wins many without compromising with evil is really what today's discouraged workers are seeking. When will they see it happen? Where will they see it? They have a right to ask! If Christians receive power after the Holy Spirit comes upon them (Acts 1:8), it is time we see the power in the lives of those who preach it!

New books about the ministry of the Holy Spirit are being written, and old books on the subject are being reprinted. This is a very encouraging development, but are we just hearing speech without seeing power? Many of us have known the mighty power of God in our ministries. We can relate true stories about the Lord saving sinners, reviving churches, restoring backsliders, and using unworthy vessels; but are we seeing God's power at work in our lives now? It is time to move from speech to power. Let us do what we ought to do to have God's blessing today.

Whence comes the power of God? I Corinthians 2 points to humility and faith as keys to having the power of God (vv. 1–5). Chapter 3 emphasizes laboring "*together with God*" (v. 9). As we have mentioned, Chapter 4 begins a section about church discipline. Holiness is one key to God's power. Of course, holiness involves separation from evil and consecration to God. Churches are to discipline their membership in order to maintain holiness and to have God's blessing. Chapters 4 and 5 give us three correct responses to "sin in the camp." As the leaders of Fundamentalist churches seek to restore the power of God to their congregations, let them employ all three as needed.

A Rod (I Corinthians 4:21)

As we have seen, this term must refer to God's power upon a preacher in his stand against sin in the church. It seems clear that it is associated with preaching. Look at the warning Paul gave in II Corinthians 12:19–21.

> *Again, think ye that we excuse ourselves unto you? we*
> *speak before God in Christ: but we do all things, dearly be-*
> *loved, for your edifying. For I fear, lest, when I come, I shall*
> *not find you such as I would, and that I shall be found unto*
> *you such as ye would not: lest there be debates, envyings,*
> *wraths, strifes, backbitings, whisperings, swellings, tumults:*
> *and lest, when I come again, my God will humble me among*
> *you, and that I shall bewail many which have sinned al-*
> *ready, and have not repented of the uncleanness and forni-*
> *cation and lasciviousness which they have committed.*

Paul threatens to *"bewail many which have sinned,"* and he will do it if he finds the congregation full of sin. This is preaching against sin with divine unction.

Church discipline begins with Spirit-anointed preaching against sin. God blesses the denunciation of sin—not only of the wicked ways of the world but also of the sins of the people staring up at the pulpit! If more of this were happening, less of the other forms of discipline would be needed in the churches.

Unfortunately, too often pastors have been pressured into being no more than activity directors, peacekeepers, and professors. A pastor ought to love his flock more than his own life, but he ought to love them enough to talk with the people plainly about their sins.

Do not Christians today need some admonition about their clothing? Nakedness is allowed by many Christian homes and even at church activities. There are plenty of Scriptures that call for both male and female modesty, and many that reprove nakedness. Is there no need for the use of those Scriptures in our pulpits?

Gender distinction is being destroyed by our society's push in the direction of homosexuality. That's why the differences between the sexes should be scripturally affirmed in the churches by their dress standards, ministry roles, and activity plans. There are Bible verses to help us in this area, and we should preach on them. Shouldn't we address the issues that are before us? Is preaching too controversial if it is biblical?

Children seldom appreciate a spanking when it is being administered! Of course the use of the rod in preaching is controversial, but it is also necessary in the pursuit of holiness.

Are we avoiding the issues of family structure? Because the world denies authority in the home, will we just go along? By silence, the pulpit spares the rod, and the pastor abuses the parishioner. Are there no sins to expose and denounce? Is there no need to call for repentance?

Christians have been swayed to indulge in all sorts of sinful entertainment in recent years. Many of them are gambling and drinking. Many more are enjoying video filth or audio carnality. Must not their pastor apply the rod? Will not the pollution of minds hinder revival in the churches?

Sins of omission abound in our unrevived churches. Cannot their pastors awaken the people to the wickedness of not praying, not giving, not witnessing, and not living for Christ?

I Corinthians 5 deals with a case of continuing fornication in the church membership. Have we such cases in our churches? Do young people come to our services for years without hearing warnings against adultery, lying, blasphemy, and stealing? What awful sins continue in our churches unrebuked. Is there really any reason to wonder why we do not see revival? Preaching against sin may not make a church popular at first, but it could make it holy and then powerful. And a holy, powerful church will eventually draw many to Christ.

Mourning (I Corinthians 5:1–2)

> It is reported commonly that there is fornication among you, and such fornication as is not so much as named among the Gentiles, that one should have his father's wife. And ye are puffed up, and have not rather mourned, that he that hath done this deed might be taken away from among you.

We could at least mourn about the sin among us. Holy weeping often leads to holiness. Read what Paul wrote in II Corinthians 7:11.

> *For behold this selfsame thing, that ye sorrowed after a godly sort, what carefulness it wrought in you, yea, what clearing of yourselves, yea, what indignation, yea, what fear, yea, what vehement desire, yea, what zeal, yea, what revenge! In all things ye have approved yourselves to be clear in this matter.*

We should mourn about our own sin.

> *Draw nigh to God, and he will draw nigh to you. Cleanse your hands, ye sinners; and purify your hearts, ye double minded. Be afflicted, and mourn, and weep: let your laughter be turned to mourning, and your joy to heaviness. Humble yourselves in the sight of the Lord, and he shall lift you up* (James 4:8–10).

We should mourn about our brother's sin and seek to restore him from carnality to spirituality.

> *Brethren, if a man be overtaken in a fault, ye which are spiritual, restore such an one in the spirit of meekness; considering thyself, lest thou also be tempted. Bear ye one another's burdens, and so fulfil the law of Christ* (Galatians 6:1–2).

We should mourn about the sin in the world.

> *Rivers of waters run down mine eyes, because they keep not thy law* (Psalm 119:136).

The psalmist wept not for the consequences of sin in men's lives, but for the sin itself! What a grief to the pure heart is the awful transgression of God's Law on the right hand and on the left. Let us mourn to holiness!

Purging (I Corinthians 5:3–8)

In a church where there is preaching against sin and mourning for sin, much sin is removed or restrained. However, every man of God and every congregation at some time or another must actually purge sin out! Such times are times of testing. Will you be loyal to God or will you be moved from holiness by an unworthy human attachment?

> *Know ye not that a little leaven leaveneth the whole*
> *lump? Purge out therefore the old leaven, that ye may be a*
> *new lump, as ye are unleavened. For even Christ our passover*
> *is sacrificed for us* (vv. 6–7).

The first young person we had to expel from our Christian school was a boy whose family was very dear to me. There was no doubt about the necessity of the action, but my part in it was performed with a broken heart. As I reflect upon that performance of duty and its consequences, I can see that the moral and spiritual tone of our school has been affected positively as a result of it. I can also see that in the experience was a test.

Some years ago a man much admired by preachers seemed to deceive us in order to cover up an embarrassing situation. In a published response to his accusers, the man made a statement; the truthfulness of that statement turned on the definition of the word *is*. To some, this pretense was obvious, but to others it was not enough to "break" with the man. Several years later, preachers expressed disgust at President Clinton's similar perversion of the word *is*, but most of us failed to see the irony in it. Such experiences with the misdeeds of colleagues in God's work are also tests of our loyalty to truth.

Good Christians must act to disassociate themselves from evil.

> *And have no fellowship with the unfruitful works of darkness, but rather reprove them* (Ephesians 5:11).

We must purge some things out of our lives in order to be holy. We must purge some things out of our churches in order to have the smile of God's countenance. We must purge things out of our sphere of approval in order to be right with God. Such purging will call for repentance. It may call for disciplinary action against church members who will not respond to preaching or the tearful entreaties of their brethren. It may mean a public break with a brother in the ministry. Purging can be emotionally difficult, but it can also be what is absolutely required to have the power of God.

We must keep talking about revival. We ought to continue to write and read about the Holy Spirit and about evangelism. But above all we must pay the price to know and experience the mighty power of God! Let us offer "*not the speech of them which are puffed up*," but rather true revival power.

> *For the kingdom of God is not in word, but in power*
> (I Corinthians 4:20).

CHAPTER 5

The Fundamentalist Approach

And Joshua said unto the people, Sanctify yourselves: for tomorrow the LORD will do wonders among you. (Joshua 3:5)

Stated in this Bible verse is the approach to the challenges of sin and evangelism that has characterized the Christian Fundamentalist movement from its beginning. It is the scriptural way to fulfill the Great Commission. It represents a philosophy of spiritual warfare that must be revived among God's servants today.

The third chapter of the Book of Joshua opens by telling us that Joshua and the children of Israel "*removed from Shittim, and came to Jordan.*" They had been at Shittim in the plains of Moab since the twenty-second chapter of Numbers. It was a place of compromise with evil, of idolatry, and of awful sin among the Lord's people. Read the record:

> *And Israel abode in Shittim, and the people began to commit whoredom with the daughters of Moab. And they called the people unto the sacrifices of their gods: and the people did eat, and bowed down to their gods* (Numbers 25:1–2).

In Numbers 31 we read that the Midianite women had *"caused the children of Israel, through the counsel of Balaam, to commit trespass against the LORD"* (v. 16). It was Balaam the erring prophet who led the Israelites into religious and moral compromise at this final camping place of their wilderness wanderings (see Numbers 33:48–49). Now a year or so later, they moved from Shittim, the place of compromise and sin, to the banks of the Jordan River, the border of Canaan. Canaan and its conquest represent in the Bible the trials and victories (as well as the defeats) of the Christian life. The passage through Jordan pictures what baptism pictures: the reckoning of oneself as dead to sin but alive to God (Romans 6:1–14), which is the formula of the true Christian life. So in Joshua 3, the Lord's people move from the place of compromise and sin to the border of the true Christian life. Their leader's marching orders at this point were *"Sanctify yourselves: for tomorrow the LORD will do wonders among you"* (v. 5).

We must note that the admonition was not to "Canaanize yourselves: for we are entering a new era of our experience!" They were not counseled to adopt Canaanite ways in order to deal with the Canaanites in whose land they were to dwell.

Let us notice also that they were not told to "unify yourselves: for we will see what great things we can do together!" Joshua and Israel were not to see what great things they could do; they were desirous of seeing the wonders that God could do!

The Fundamentalists of the twentieth century were characterized by adherence to the principle of separation from evil. Bible students all know that the concepts of sanctification and holiness in both Testaments are centered on the concept of separation unto God. Holy places and holy things were consecrated to the Lord–separated from profane things so that they could be dedicated solely to His use. Sanctification involves the kind of separation required by the marriage commitment. A man is separated from all other women so that he can freely enjoy a loving relationship with his wife. Wrongful involvement with others will ruin love in a marriage; the bride and groom must separate from all others for the sake of their union. In such a way, believers are to separate from evil in order to enjoy a relationship of unhindered fellowship and blessing with God. This is biblical separation and biblical sanctification at the core.

Fundamentalists have necessarily tended to be separatists. The term *Fundamentalist* means that they define Christianity in terms of certain fundamental doctrines. These essential truths make up the Christian Faith itself. True Christians may differ on lesser doctrines, but they must agree with the fundamentals in order to be Christians. In other words, Fundamentalists say that the fundamentals are fundamental to the Faith! Of course, the word *fundamental* means "basic or essential."

Fundamentalists say that belief in the infallibility of the Bible, the deity of Christ, His substitutionary atonement, His bodily resurrection, and justification through faith in Him alone are fundamental and therefore essential to real Christianity. An "evangelical" by definition believes in these gospel doctrines, but he does not necessarily insist that they are "fundamental" to the Faith. Non-Fundamentalist evangelicals concede that liberals can be Christians. Either they say it, or they act in a way to indicate their belief that certain infidels are true Christians–by including them in cooperative evangelism, by keeping them on denominational salaries, or by joining them in ministerial or church associations. Fundamentalists refuse to recognize liberals as Christians because they deny certain fundamentals of the Faith. Fundamentalism, therefore, demands a certain degree of separatism because of what it means. Therefore the Fundamentalist approach to the issues and challenges of the day was to "*sanctify* [separate] *yourselves: for tomorrow the LORD will do wonders among you*" (Joshua 3:5).

During and after the Second World War, a new direction away from separation grew popular among American Fundamentalists. It came to be known as the "New Evangelicalism," but it began as a new approach to evangelism that seemed to sweep the field. The leaders of this movement were convinced that the methods and trappings of evangelism in the past had become offensive to modern-day Americans and were obstacles to effective soulwinning. For the new generation, preachers would have to be more positive, music would have to be lighter and more exciting, language would have to be more secular, standards would have to be more accommodating, and ministerial training would have to be more extensive among evangelicals. By 1950, some of the leaders and followers of this new direction had rejected separation from liberalism altogether. Now they were advocating the infiltration of liberal-controlled denominations, associations, and councils, rather than separation from them. This approach was in direct contradiction to New Testament teaching, of course.

> *And have no fellowship with the unfruitful works of darkness, but rather reprove them* (Ephesians 5:11).

> *Be ye not unequally yoked together with unbelievers: for what fellowship hath righteousness with unrighteousness? and what communion hath light with darkness? And what concord hath Christ with Belial? or what part hath he that believeth with an infidel?* (II Corinthians 6:14–15).

The mood for this unscriptural trend was set by the approach that we must Canaanize ourselves as we enter Canaan! This idea has been taken to awful extremes now that we have entered the twenty-first century. Evangelical organizations and churches will do almost anything to look, sound, and act like the world. They want to join sinners in order to win them. Yet we again would ask, "If the church now talks, walks, sings, and dresses like the world, who is winning whom?" The evangelistic crusades of the latter twentieth century, although big and spectacular, were colossal failures as far as affecting the culture is concerned! The New Evangelical approach was wrong from its inception, and the Fundamentalist approach, although a harder road to travel, was essentially right! "*Sanctify yourselves: for tomorrow the LORD will do wonders among you*" (Joshua 3:5).

After an explosion of evangelism in the separatist Fundamentalist churches during the 1960s and '70s, certain men saw political power in the great mass of new converts. The channeling of this multitude into conservative-Republican activism brought about the nomination and election of Mr. Reagan as President in 1980.

However, this worldly victory did not come without paying a price in the separation of truth from error. Fundamentalists organized with Mormons, Roman Catholics, Jews, and Moonies to champion the causes of human life, public piety, smaller government, and international anti-Communism. The idea that certain men promoted incessantly was that great good could be done if moral people would just work together! Doctrinal differences, they indicated, were but petty prejudices that hindered the cause of righteousness. The truth is that amazing political achievements were accomplished by the moral crusade of those days; but while the Reagan era moved the nation politically to the right, its culture slipped morally and spiritually to new lows. The concept of unifying for power was a failure in the long run. We should have followed the command, "*Sanctify yourselves: for tomorrow the LORD will do wonders among you*" (Joshua 3:5).

Now the Fundamentalist movement as a whole is in danger of losing its moorings. The reasons behind the approach of our spiritual fathers have been misunderstood by many and forgotten by many more. A growing number of Fundamentalists are seeing no point in separation. A group of others are growing colder each year. Some churches are seeking to fake revival by the use of carnal music and worldly entertainment to gather and excite great crowds. Other churches are maintaining high standards, but they don't seem to remember why. Some of these have given up on revival. They remind us of a marriage in which the couple are technically faithful to each other but do not love each other any more. There are two dangerous departures from the Fundamentalist approach that present themselves to believers today: (1) seeking wonders without promoting sanctification and (2) promoting sanctification without seeking wonders.

Seeking Wonders without Promoting Sanctification

Joshua told the people, "*Sanctify yourselves: for tomorrow the LORD will do wonders among you*" (Joshua 3:5). In other words, they were to please God so that He would be willing to work in a supernatural way on their behalf. The same concept is found in the New Testament Scriptures.

> *Draw nigh to God, and he will draw nigh to you. Cleanse your hands, ye sinners; and purify your hearts, ye double minded. Be afflicted, and mourn, and weep: let your laughter be turned to mourning, and your joy to heaviness. Humble yourselves in the sight of the Lord, and he shall lift you up* (James 4:8–10).

> *For do I now persuade men, or God? or do I seek to please men? for if I yet pleased men, I should not be the servant of Christ* (Galatians 1:10).

We are commanded to preach the gospel to "every creature" in the world and to do this work in the power of the Holy Spirit (Acts 1:8; I Corinthians 2:4–5). We are promised fruit in this endeavor, generated by God's power working in us (John 15:5; Colossians 1:29). If a soul is won to Christ, a miracle has happened: the dead has been brought to life! To think that raising the dead can be accomplished by appealing to the tastes of dead men is absurd. Raising the dead requires the power of God. It is God that must be pleased in evangelistic work—not men.

Those who want to see "wonders" without sanctifying themselves are missing this point. They are attracted to schemes that minimize or omit seeking the blessing of God, and they concentrate on appealing to the interests and viewpoints of sinners. Fundamentalists and evangelicals of every stripe have fallen into the trap of seeking results without revival. Sometimes they want to call it "revival" when they get the results they seek, but without holiness there has been no real revival. Both personal and ecclesiastical separation (sanctification) are essential to having the blessing of God. You cannot really seek His face without turning from your wicked ways (II Chronicles 7:14). When we yoke up with infidels to reach their congregations, when we use sensual music to bring in the young, and when we fashion our message to coincide with current ways of thinking, we have abandoned any real interest in pleasing the true and living God or conforming to His will. We may meet with some outward success, but we will never see the "wonders" God promised to a sanctified people.

Promoting Sanctification without Seeking Wonders

Fundamentalists that refuse to fake revival these days are often persuaded to deny it! Two common and popular errors taught by preachers today are (1) that revival is not possible in this day of apostasy and (2) that revival is a sovereign act of God that should never be sought and can never be actually expected. Many of those who deny that God has promised to revive His people in response to their repentance and faith are separatists. They refuse to recognize liberals as Christians. They refuse to bring carnal and worldly music into the church. They live by certain standards of personal holiness. Yet they expect nothing from God in answer to this sanctification. But Joshua expected "wonders"! "*Sanctify yourselves: for tomorrow the LORD will do wonders among you*" (Joshua 3:5).

What actually is the purpose of sanctifying oneself, in the sense of separating one's life from evil? Few believe that it is to maintain the state of grace. Our motivation for shunning sin is not to stay saved. Ultimately, it is to please God, to be sure. We are to be conformed to the image of Christ. Yet this final form of sanctification will come at the glorification of our bodies, and it will happen without any effort on our part. Our sanctification in this life will be incomplete at best, while at the coming of Jesus it will be total and certain. We are not avoiding evil and its appearance or fellowship with the works of darkness in order to keep our salvation or to achieve some imperfect Christlikeness. We seek to be holy unto the Lord for the purpose of being used of Him to accomplish wonderful things to His glory! In the Old Testament, revived Israel won wars and conquered kingdoms; in the New Testament age, revived Christians win souls to Christ and overcome the Devil and his cohorts. We must sanctify ourselves and expect to see wonders.

Basically, Fundamentalism has always been a revival movement. Its emphasis is properly vertical rather than improperly horizontal. We separate ourselves from the evil of this world in order to seek the power and blessing of God in our service for Him. When Fundamentalists lose their passion for revival, they lose an important aspect of their Fundamentalism. Faith in the Bible's promise of revival is the right motive for separation. No other motive will stand. Let us return to the approach commanded by Joshua as we continue the fight for the Faith! As we separate ourselves from evil, let Fundamentalists seek the face of God for the bestowal of great wonders!

CHAPTER 6

Will It Do Any Good to Pray?

If ye then, being evil, know how to give good gifts unto your children: how much more shall your heavenly Father give the Holy Spirit to them that ask him? (Luke 11:13)

The whole point of emphasizing the need for revival is to encourage God's people to ask Him for it! Revival is something God does. There is no dispute over that. The question of whether He does it as a sovereign act or as a promised response does not involve whether God does it or not. God must "*revive us again*" (Psalm 85) if we are to be revived. Since we must seek the Lord for revival, prayer is indispensable to it. Yet the faith of many is failing in regard to the effectiveness of prayer for revival. Some sadly say that they have been praying for months or for years for revival with no results. And it is for this reason that many conclude that it does no good to pray for revival!

Yet praying for revival is largely what Fundamentalists are not doing to address the problems of worldliness and carnality in their churches. The revival prayer meeting is largely "a thing of the past" among Fundamentalists! What our forefathers did to seek the blessing of God, compared with what little we do today, reveals why we see little of His blessing today. Some talk about praying for revival, but few watch and pray, fast and pray, or unite with others in seasons of prayer for revival. Those who do pray often offer hindered prayers. Some pray in ignorance of God's truth about revival's requirements. Others try to pray in faith without works. Those who would expect the ministry of the Holy Ghost must also obey God according to Acts 5:32. *"We are his witnesses of these things; and so is also the Holy Ghost, whom God hath given to them that obey him."*

However, the Bible gives us great encouragement that the Lord will indeed revive His people in answer to earnest prayer!

> *Cast not away therefore your confidence, which hath great recompense of reward* (Hebrews 10:35).

> *Turn us, O God of our salvation, and cause thine anger toward us to cease. Wilt thou be angry with us for ever? wilt thou draw out thine anger to all generations? Wilt thou not revive us again: that thy people may rejoice in thee?* (Psalm 85:4–6)

The Promise of the Spirit

Luke 11 contains a promise spoken by the Lord Jesus that is one of the most hotly debated verses in the New Testament. Luke 11:13 concludes and summarizes a record of one of Christ's lessons on prayer.

> *If ye then, being evil, know how to give good gifts unto your children: how much more shall your heavenly Father give the Holy Spirit to them that ask him?*

Several things about the Greek grammar of this verse clarify its meaning, but a study of the doctrine of the Holy Spirit in Luke and Acts is also necessary in understanding what Jesus was promising.

The narratives of the books of Luke and Acts (written, of course, by the same penman) often teach us about the ministry of the Spirit and help us define important terms. The first chapter of Luke says of John the Baptist,

> *He shall be filled with the Holy Ghost, even from his mother's womb. And many of the children of Israel shall he turn to the Lord their God. And he shall go before him in the spirit and power of Elias, to turn the hearts of the fathers to the children, and the disobedient to the wisdom of the just; to make ready a people prepared for the Lord* (vv. 15b–17).

Here we learn something of what it means to be "filled" with God's Spirit.

In the third chapter, John the Baptist speaks of Jesus when he says, "*He shall baptize you with the Holy Ghost*" (v. 16b). Here we meet the term "*baptize you with the Holy Ghost.*"

In verse 22 of Luke 3, "*the Holy Ghost descended*" upon Jesus at His baptism, and after this occurrence, "*Jesus being full of the Holy Ghost returned from Jordan, and was led by the Spirit into the wilderness*" (Luke 4:1).

After His wilderness temptation, "*Jesus returned in the power of the Spirit into Galilee: and there went out a fame of him through all the region round about*" (Luke 4:14–15).

In Nazareth, He opened the Scripture at a synagogue and "*found the place where it was written, The Spirit of the Lord is upon me, because he hath anointed me to preach the gospel to the poor*" (Luke 4:17b–18a).

Then He said, "*This day is this scripture fulfilled in your ears*" (Luke 4:21).

The response of the people is recorded as follows: "*And all bare him witness, and wondered at the gracious words which proceeded out of his mouth. And they said, Is not this Joseph's son?*" (Luke 4:22).

The power of the Holy Spirit upon Him was evident to all the people. Up through the fourth chapter of Luke we have learned several terms involved in the New Testament teaching about the Holy Spirit: filled with the Spirit (1:15; 4:1), baptized with the Spirit (3:16), the Spirit coming or being upon someone (3:22; 4:18), being led by the Spirit (4:1), and coming in the power of the Spirit (4:14). Indications are that several of these terms refer to the same experience. Also, it is clear that one filled with the Holy Spirit has the power to preach the gospel effectively and to turn men to God.

In the following chapters, the reader becomes familiar with "the power of the Lord" in the life and ministry of the Lord Jesus through the filling of the Spirit: "*and the power of the Lord was present*" (5:17b).

In Acts 10:38, this power is described this way: "*God anointed Jesus of Nazareth with the Holy Ghost and with power: who went about doing good, and healing all that were oppressed of the devil; for God was with him.*"

Then in Luke 11, Jesus talks to His disciples about having the same power in their own lives and about how prayer is the key. The whole subject of Luke 11:1–13 is prayer (note verse 1).

In His teaching, the Lord gives again the "model prayer" as an example of how to pray daily (vv. 2–4). Then He tells the Parable of the Persistent Friend (vv. 5–8) and shows us that continuance in praying for certain things is important to getting them (the point also of Luke 18:1–8). This teaching continues through the promise of verse 13.

> *If ye then, being evil, know how to give good gifts unto your children: how much more shall your heavenly Father give the Holy Spirit to them that ask him?*

The Essence of the Spirit

The controversial part of this verse is God's promise to "*give the Holy Spirit to them that ask him.*" What did Jesus mean by this? Some of the meaning of this promise is in the Greek grammar.

In the original, "*the Holy Spirit*" in Luke 11:13 lacks the article. In English we can have the definite ("the") or the indefinite ("a") article before a noun, or no article at all. In Greek (the original language of the New Testament) there is simply the article or no article. The use of the article in Greek is entirely different from the use of the article in English. It is not easy to know exactly how to render Greek into English when there is some article peculiarity. Usually the translator will use the English indefinite article when the article is absent in Greek and the definite article in English when the Greek article is used. However, the meaning is not really that simple.

Dana and Mantey's *Manual Grammar of the Greek New Testament* says, "Sometimes with a noun which the context proves to be definite the article is not used. This places stress upon the qualitative aspect of the noun rather than its mere identity. An object of thought may be conceived at from two points of view: as to identity or quality. To convey the first point of view the Greek uses the article; for the second the anarthrous construction [without the article] is used."[1]

In other words, when there is no article, the sentence is emphasizing the quality of the noun rather than its identity. It is not so much about what the thing is or which thing it is as it is about the essence or the quality of the thing! Therefore Luke 11:13 means that the Father will give the essence of the Holy Spirit to those who ask. In the context of the Book of Luke, this would mean the ministry and power of the Spirit that the disciples had seen in the Lord's life.

Making It Simple

Ephesians 1:12–14 and 4:30 teach us that every believer in Jesus Christ has been sealed with the Holy Spirit "*unto the day of redemption.*" Every Christian then has the Holy Spirit living within him (see also John 14:15–17; Romans 8:9; I Corinthians 6:19). However, Ephesians 5:18 commands people who are already sealed with the Spirit to be filled with the Spirit! Although the presence of the Holy Spirit came automatically when we trusted Christ for our salvation (whether we knew it or not), the full ministry of the Spirit in our lives does not happen automatically. Galatians 3 makes it clear that our spiritual growth, as well as our salvation, comes from the Holy Spirit, and that it comes by faith (not by flesh-energized works) just as salvation does.

> *This only would I learn of you, Received ye the Spirit by the works of the law, or by the hearing of faith? Are ye so*

foolish? having begun in the Spirit, are ye now made perfect by the flesh? (vv. 2–3).

Faith in Christ accesses the power of the Spirit for true Christian living and service.

> *I am crucified with Christ: nevertheless I live; yet not I, but Christ liveth in me: and the life which I now live in the flesh I live by the faith of the Son of God, who loved me, and gave himself for me* (Galatians 2:20).

Yet Christians often struggle with the meaning of living and serving by faith and with the submission to Christ that such a life requires. This is why Christ made it simple for us. He said that God would grant us the ministry of His Spirit in its fullness if we would earnestly ask Him to do it!

The teaching about the Spirit in the Book of Acts shows us that often prayer leads to the Spirit's power. Find a ten-day prayer meeting before the coming of the Spirit on the Day of Pentecost in Acts 1 and 2. Find another prayer meeting before a new filling of the church in Acts 4. Find another prayer meeting before the renewed multiplication of the church in Acts 6. Find Saul of Tarsus praying before he is filled with the Spirit in Acts 9. These examples of prayer before power reflect the role of prayer in the filling of the Lord Jesus back in Luke 3.

> *Now when all the people were baptized, it came to pass, that Jesus also being baptized, and praying, the heaven was opened, and the Holy Ghost descended in a bodily shape like a dove upon him, and a voice came from heaven, which said, Thou art my beloved Son; in thee I am well pleased* (vv. 21–22).

Notice that Luke says Jesus was "praying" as He was being baptized and filled with the Spirit.

Our promise in Luke 11:13 encourages us to pray for the full ministry of the Spirit in our lives! God has simplified the requirements of faith and submission by telling us to pray for the quality or essence of the Holy Ghost. As we pray, we learn to submit and believe, and thus meet the requirements.

Keep Asking

The tense of the Greek word for "ask" in this verse is also very important to understanding the promise. It is a present participle, which indicates continuous action. In other words, God promises the ministry of the Spirit to those who are continually asking for it. The present tense in the verbs of verses 9 and 10 speak of continuous asking, seeking, and knocking. The idea is "be asking" or "keep on asking" and you will surely receive. This is certainly the lesson of the parable in verses 5 through 8. It was "importunity" (shameless persistence) that got a friend what he wanted from his friend. Persistent, earnest, continuing, and insistent prayer, based on the promise of God, is what will obtain good things from the heavenly Father.

Jesus further encourages us to keep on praying for the power of the Spirit by saying, "*How much more shall your heavenly Father give the Holy Spirit to them that ask him?*"

The Father is more than willing to give a believer the fullness of His Spirit if that believer will continually and humbly beseech Him for it! "How much more" is God willing to do this for us than we are to give good gifts to our own children! Throughout the Book of Acts this promise is demonstrated to be true. God gave the baptism of the Spirit (Acts 1:4–5), which apparently was the same as having "*the Holy Ghost come upon you*" (Acts 1:8) and being "*filled with the Holy Ghost*" (Acts 2:4), in response to ten days of united, continual, heart-searching prayer (Acts 1:14–2:4).

Peter said that this was the fulfillment of God's promise to "*pour out*" His Spirit (Acts 2:15–18) and that it could be called to "*receive the gift of the Holy Ghost*" (Acts 2:38–39). His words referred directly to the promise of Luke 11:13. The Father has promised to give the fullness of the Spirit to them that continually ask Him for it. It is a gift to be received!

In Acts 8, the apostles Peter and John came to the new converts of Samaria and "*prayed for them, that they might receive the Holy Ghost*" (v. 15). This is another reference to the promise of Luke 11:13, and again the article is absent before the words *Holy*

Ghost in Greek. They were not praying for the sealing of the Spirit, which had already happened, but rather for the essence or power of the Spirit!

It should thrill us all that God has promised to put us into the state of true revival in answer to our beseeching prayer! The term "filled with the Spirit," as well as the other terms related to it in Luke/Acts, is a description of the Christian at the normal level of spiritual life and power. Being lifted up to the normal is by definition the experience of revival!

This is why praying for revival makes good sense. In fact, it is only right that Christian men and women seek the Lord in prayer when their lives and their churches are sunk into carnality, disobedience, and worldliness! But we do not pray without hope, for Jesus promised that the Father will give revival to those who will be asking Him for it! In this day of discouragement, unbelief, and rampant sin in many Fundamentalist churches, let there be a renewal of prayer for revival. Let preachers set aside days of fasting or nights of watching in prayer for revival. Let individual Christians of every calling make revival and matters involved in it prominent subjects of petition in their private devotions! Let churchwide prayer meetings be called to seek God for revival, and let the people assemble regularly until revival comes! Let churches of like faith come together for revival prayer meetings! Let us believe God and seek Him for what we need!

During the Second Great Awakening in America, an evangelist related this encouraging story about prayer for revival: "In a certain town there had been no revival for many years; the church was nearly run out, the youth were all unconverted, and desolation reigned unbroken. There lived in a retired part of the town, an aged man, a blacksmith by trade, and of so stammering a tongue, that it was painful to hear him speak. On one Friday, as he was at work in his shop, alone, his mind became greatly exercised about the state of the church, and of the impenitent. His agony became so great, that he was induced to lay by his work, lock the shop door, and spend the afternoon in prayer.

"He prevailed, and on the Sabbath called on the minister, and desired him to appoint a conference meeting. After some hesitation, the minister consented, observing, however, that he feared but few would attend. He appointed it the same evening, at a large private house. When evening came, more assembled than could be accommodated in the house. All was silent for a time, until one sinner broke out in tears, and said, if any one could pray, he begged him to pray for him. Another followed, and another, and still another, until it was found that persons from every quarter of the town were under deep conviction. And what was remarkable was that they all dated their conviction at the hour when the old man was praying in his shop. A powerful revival followed. Thus this old stammering man prevailed, and, as a prince, had power with God."[2]

Certainly, my friends, prayer is the way!

NOTES

[1]H. E. Dana and Julius Road Mantey, *A Manual Grammar of the Greek New Testament* (New York: The Macmillan Company, 1927), p. 149.

[2]Charles G. Finney, *Lectures on Revivals of Religion* (New York: Fleming H. Revell Company, 1868), p. 65.